Also by Darrell Bourque

Plainsongs
The Doors Between Us
Burnt Water Suite
The Blue Boat
Call and Response: Conversations in Verse (with Jack Bedell)
In Ordinary Light: New and Selected Poems
Megan's Guitar and Other Poems from Acadie
From the Other Side: Henriette Delille
if you abandon me, *comment je vas faire*: An Amédé Ardoin Songbook
Where I Waited
migraré

Until We Talk

Until We Talk

Darrell Bourque and Bill Gingles

Etruscan Press

Etruscan Press
Wilkes University
84 West South Street
Wilkes-Barre, PA 18766
(570) 408-4546

www.etruscanpress.org

Published 2023 by Etruscan Press
Printed in the United States of America
Cover art: *Until We Talk*, 2022 © Bill Gingles
Cover design by Jess Morandi
Interior design and typesetting by Aaron Petrovich
The text of this book is set in Didot

First Edition

17 18 19 20 5 4 3 2 1

Library of Congress Cataloging-in-Publication Data

Names: Bourque, Darrell, 1942– author. | Gingles, Bill, 1958– illustrator.
Title: Until we talk / Darrell Bourque and Bill Gingles.
Description: First edition. | Wilkes-Barre, PA : Etruscan Press, 2023. | Summary: "UNTIL
    WE TALK is a set of jazz-inflected ghazals tied to epigraphs from Colum McCann's
    novel APEIROGON and illuminated with Bill Gingles's abstract expressionist paintings.
    Predominately rooted in the tragic losses in contemporary Israeli and Palestinian families,
    the poems braid those losses into parallel losses in geopolitical race, ethnic, class, and caste
    conflicts"-- Provided by publisher.
Identifiers: LCCN 2022035943 | ISBN 9798985882414 (trade paperback)
Subjects: LCGFT: Poetry.
Classification: LCC PS3602.O89275 U58 2023 | DDC 811/.6--dc23/eng/20220908
LC record available at https://lccn.loc.gov/2022035943

Please turn to the back of this book for a list of the sustaining funders of Etruscan Press.

This book is printed on recycled, acid-free paper.

for daughters and sons, husbands and wives, fathers and mothers, parents and grandparents, aunts, uncles and cousins, for our neighbors, teachers, friends and relations, for everyone who resists the diminishment, supremacy and silence inside the constructs of territories, occupations, plantations, internment camps, settlements, reservations, residential schools, gulags and ghettos by whatever names they are called.

CONTENTS

FOREWORD
Darrell Bourque

One story becoming another. (Canto 19, p 447)

We begin our lives inside a story. We are most often not the object or the driver of the story of our beginning. We begin as this dividing cell inside the lives of others who know nothing of what we are, of what we are to become. The drivers of the story are various: geography, eros, culture, desire, history, lust, tradition, proximity, urge, accident, crime. But those of us who do make it here make the journey into the world of storytellers and our story becomes another story.

When I first read Colum McCann's *Apeirogon*, I cannot tell you what I was most taken with. There was the magic of an incredible structure not unlike the Minbar of Saladin or the "no glue, no nails" stories Scheherazade tells to save not only her own life and her sister's, but the lives of the women of the kingdom, as well as the humanity of the powerful King Shahryar. And, there was the story of these two fathers, one Israeli and one Palestinian, whose loss of their young daughters change them into peace makers. Facing grief head on and then going beyond grief catapults each of them into a story they could not have imagined, nor one they would have invited with the horrific circumstances that turn them heroic even if they might shrink from a label that hardly has a place in their stories as they see them.

Then, when I read the novel again, Rami Elhanan and Bassam Aramin's daughters, Smadar and Abir, became my daughters. Nurit Peled Elhanan and Salwa Aramin emerged as distinctly different but distinctly strong women of their time, mothers and independent thinkers, each one so connected to her own history and geography and culture, and each one a guide to the kind of resilience and love and commitment to the forces of clarity that have nearly always changed histories and geographies and cultures the world over. Each one of these women, a powerful story in her own right.

It was in this second and subsequent readings that I could see that this story Colum McCann was telling was one story becoming another. I was reading this story as I was trying to absorb the horror of the death of George Floyd, Breonna Taylor, Philando Castile and Sandra Bland, with echoes of the deaths of Tamir Rice, Michael Brown, Trayvon Martin and so many others still ringing in me. I was reading and rereading writers like Natalie Diaz and Ernest J. Gaines, Joy Harjo and Toni Morrison, James Baldwin and Naomi Shihab Nye, Yusef Komunyakaa and Sherman Alexi, Lucille Clifton and Thomas Merton, Luis Urrea and Louise Erdrich, all offering us ways beyond the debilitating prescriptives of colonialism. I was being introduced to the works of Edward Said, the poetry of Darwish; reintroduced to Borges. I was thinking of the ways in which we have been telling ourselves since the 70s that we live in a post-colonial time while we see that texts like the Papal Bulls of the 15th century, and other seminal texts, still guide the neocolonial politics of our own time.

The stories in this story told in ghazals are parallel stories connected to internments, sieges, settlements, reservations, slavery, plantation mentalities and erasures of every kind. The stories here link themselves to generational and historical traumas wherever they occur. The story here is the story of the Me Too Movement as it is the story of Black Lives Matter Movement. It is a story for human rights, against calcifying fear and calcifying power, about social justice, and against Occupation wherever and however it shows itself.

When we enter the story, we change it. That's a matter of simple physics. When we let stories come at us fully and mindfully, it's as though our lives depended on them, as though our survival depended on them. It's with this conviction that I began to write the 52 poems in this collection.

FOREWORD
Bill Gingles

When Darrell called to tell me about his idea for this book, I felt at once delighted and daunted by the prospect of pairing paintings I'd already painted to poems not yet written. As he laid out his vision for the book, it became pretty clear pretty quickly that this was not going to be easy, but I knew I wanted to be a part of such a beautiful endeavor.

Since the paintings and poems were not originally keyed to each other, the challenge was to find a way to pair them in real and meaningful ways. I knew my paintings intimately but the poems, as they trickled in through the weeks, were new to me. I realized that some degree of intimacy with the poems would be necessary in order to find a way to make each pairing. This would mean living with the poems. Reading them again and again. Reading them with images of paintings in an adjacent window on my computer screen or on my studio wall nearby. Seeing the poems play out in my mind. Feeling myself a witness to the social crimes and injustices, the tragedies, and the poignant beauty that sometimes came from them.

I made myself open to suggestions by any part of the poem; the title, the epigraph, the tone, a particular phrase, or a narrative element. At least once I let the title of the poem help me decide, as in "Story" paired with *The Same Story*, but that was quite rare and I found, for the most part, I had to disregard the paintings' titles in order to find a resonance between them and the poems.

Sometimes the resonance was color. Like the yellow in the Ortolan Buntings in "To Let Them Go" and the yellow in *Intimate Dawn*. Or color and place like the gold dome in "1 of 1001 Paths to the Monastery at Beit Jala" and the gold in *Daybreak*. With "The Jericho House," I paired *Rumours of an Exit* because of the arched entrance on the left side and the enclosed greenery on the right.

One pairing that has stuck with me was "She Was Ten" paired with *This*. I could see the father carrying the picture of his murdered daughter. I could feel the pressure in the room as he pointedly slid the picture across the table for the Senator to see. This. This is my daughter. You are responsible for this. This is the loss I live with.

In the course of my work on this book, Darrell said he saw my paintings as being like illuminations, as in illuminated manuscripts. But then he said that wasn't exactly correct. Yet the more I think about it, the better that linkage sounds. My paintings shining their own light on these brilliant poems.

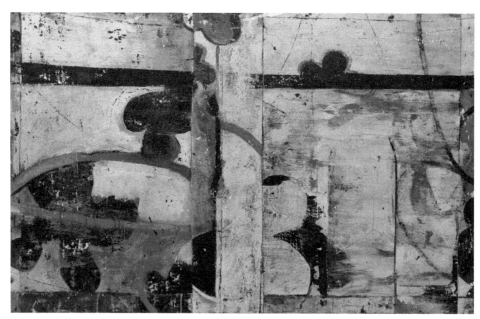

OVERSOUL'S HINT, acrylic on canvas, 3o" x 48" MMXXI

THE GHAZALS OF APEIROGON

> On the wall of the restaurant were photographs of
> frigatebirds scissoring over the sea. … To ancient
> mariners they were called Men-of-War.

Let's say we will call the shots in this world of Rilke's widening
circles and start with names of things. Why not start with birds?

Let's do the ancient mariners one better and forego Men-of-War
for the frigatebird. Birds in flight are poems so let scissoring birds

be instead *ghazals*. While we're at it, make them land birds too,
whirling heavenward then coming down again feet first. Birds

change from major to minor in midair as all those great songs do.
Storms shift like that as well. And the falcon ascending over birds

they love to fly with and then returning to the hood is prayer
and song and storm sutured in bird skin and bird bone. Birds

we call frigatebirds are death-defying in their falls. The ghazal
bird will fly over Tiersenstadt, hold pattern when other birds

veer, fly even the bloodiest of migratory paths over Palestine
and Israel. Our ghazal can take the hit of painted rocks, birds

of prey, pylons, punks, oil pits, poisons, pesticides, poachers,
can ride storms, sing, talk, and make sky lines with other birds.

HOLY FOR A MOMENT, acrylic on canvas, 3o" x 24" MMXXI

AFTER PRAYER

After the prayers, the monks would walk out the arched
doorway, down the gravel path, toward the vineyard in the
gathering dark ... They spread out around the vineyard, pouring
small circles of water around the bases of the plants.

The cream they left on shelves in the kitchen for the souring,
the first step to clotting, clabbering, and curd, then pouring

of the sweet whey they will bottle for market. Tonight they
water these vines as they do everything here. The pouring

is in small allotments. In a land as arid as this land is, a light
hand is more than called for. The sound of vespers pouring

earlier from the throats of the few monks left here is shadow
of the old sound of the hundred monks and their outpouring

of thanks for another day. To do what you are called to do
is the other side of prayer, and not the lesser side. Pouring

this water in small circles will keep more than the vines alive.
There is the holy wine, for sure, but there's also the pouring

of white habits into the fields at harvest time. The neighbor
nuns coming in to help. On dark nights their candles pouring

little spheres of light onto the fruit. The stories we house here,
so like our dented buckets, our gathering dark, our holy pouring.

COME AWAY, acrylic on canvas, 48" x 48" MMXXI

FLIGHT

Will causing pain to someone else ease
the unbearable pain that you are suffering?

About suffering they were never wrong, he tells us in this parable
of a boy making wings of waxed feathers to satisfy an unbearable

urge to fly with his father to a better place. Auden knew Breugel
who knew this boy who knew the labyrinth and how unbearable

life can be inside a maze. We fill our stories with these flying things.
Alf Layla wa-Layla takes on the cloak of one woman's unbearable

plight and fills it with flying djinns and carpets and tales from
who knows where. In the end she lives. Others' unbearable

suffering became part of the Prophet's story. Adam's, Abraham's,
Moses' and Jesus' he carried in Him. His own suffering unbearable,

he bore. Before Jesus flew into his transcendence, he suffocated
on a bloody cross. The cross was not the end. The unbearable

never is. Six million Jews, and more, emptying Tibet of Buddhists,
siege of Leningrad, the list goes on and on. To stop the unbearable

wherever we find ourselves, we cannot be wrong about suffering,
or lean away from the holy flight of stories bearing the unbearable.

ON MY WAY HERE, acrylic on canvas, 60" x 40" MMXX

INFRASTRUCTURE

We build roads above them and below them,
but only to make them faceless.

My name is Rami Elhanan. My friend is Bassam Aramin. We speak in codes,
make jokes for a place to breathe. Later I might tell you. It's not the roads

they say, or the walls, like it's not the guns that kill people, or the bombs, or
painted rocks and rubber bullets, but it's all those things we say. The roads

you build change more than geography. The cutaways and walls keeping
us from seeing each other are long divisions, not algebra. What are roads

and walls to Jericho, to Detroit, Atlanta, El Paso. Wherever you are going
you're too elevated or too submerged to see. They've built the wide roads

so you will not see Tremé, or Sugar Hill, or Greenwood. *Haven't the Jews
suffered enough.* That is but one of Bassam's jokes. He keeps infinite roads

to love in his vest. Bassam tells of friends throwing two grenades at a jeep:
two-han-d-eh-gre-nay-des. Bassam's Hebron accent can travel many roads.

Two becomes two hundred and it becomes one of our jokes. I say, "Hey,
Brother, go ahead and throw two hundred grenades." Brothers' roads

have faces others cannot see in tunnels. In tunnels darkness underscores
what light holds tenuously. With no mindful base courses, no good roads.

RECURRING DOUBT, acrylic on canvas, 16" x 12" MMXX

THE MOWER

The garden was small, so he took to mowing
the verge on the service road outside.

In the back and forth his grief would not subside but it did not surge
either. Grief repeats itself, a small prayer inside leading to the verge,

that larger prayer you did not even know you could pray. My cousin
lost his wife to the virus of the pandemic. He says he's on the verge

of madness most days. He starts up the riding lawn mower, mows
his own yard three times a week. All unmown calling like the verge

calls bishops and deans to their offices. In Bradford, that Palestinian
on scholarship in England is weeding his garden. He is on the verge

of something he could not name at home. During Festival of Sacrifice
his wife bought him gardening gloves. Today he's not mowing the verge.

He's closer to who he is inside than perhaps he's ever been. His house
is near. He hears his wife preparing *halim* and shish kebabs. A verge

of tears is about to spill from the skin around his eyes. How can want
and place and kin and loss and doubt and hope and love shape a verge

around us? Love is but one road to Palestine, *Eid al-Adha* is another.
My cousin sees his wife weeding as he is coming in from the verge.

I'M HERE, acrylic on canvas, 24" x 3o" MMXXI

WHEN NOT ENOUGH IS ALL WE HAVE

I'm not sure I can tell you exactly what I mean.
We have words but sometimes they're not enough.

The boy in the rubber raft in the wine dark sea still dreams of herds
of sheep he tended. He plays the oud. He has not found the words

yet to the song he wants to sing, but he has a plan to find them
when he gets to where he's going. Jane Pittman heard the words

Jimmy spoke before he had spoken them, could see them coming
from him like sermon, like story, like poem. He knows how words

work she told everyone in the Quarters. He will be the one. Gandhi,
Nelson, King, Malcolm, Sojourner, Bobby, Jack, Medgar — the words

were who they were. Who Harriet was, who Thurman was. *Not
enough* is what kept them wading in the rivers of parable. Words

were all Henriette Delille needed to teach slave children to read
in the Ursuline Convent she was denied admission to. A few words

and she was off to tend to those homeless Haitian women selling
paper flowers in the streets and starving still. One father's words

Here I am turned a whole story on its head. This other Abraham
saw the unthinkable of his time. He braided freedom in his words.

THE WAKING EDGE, acrylic on canvas, 40" x 60" MMXIX

CHOKEHOLDS

A community of feelings. A mythology of the instincts.

The walled precincts of death and dying are the last precincts
of the last territories we will occupy, our territory of instincts.

Voltaire went straight at the attending priest in his last rites.
Do you renounce Satan? the old priest asked. *This*, instincts

replied, *is not the time to make enemies*. George Floyd's words:
Ah! Ah! Please. Please. Please, is about faith and belief instincts

in one man with all the odds stacked up against him. The man
who tells him to stop talking says he was not going by instincts,

that this was something he was trained to do and it was his duty
guiding him that day in Minneapolis. We can wonder if instincts

also guided him when he told the dying man to stop talking,
that *It takes a heck of a lot of oxygen to talk*. Dumb instincts

do not see the small deaths in a mother in Palestine whose
head is examined with rubber gloves before her best instincts

tell her not to break down in front of her children. She is strip-
searched before they are. Their silence is a silence of instincts.

THE UNREMEMBERED GATE, acrylic on canvas, 3o" x 4o" MMXVII

WHAT THEY LOVED, BRADFORD, ENGLAND

... the lopsided gate, the yellow climbing rose along the wall, the blue
   door, the white bell, the silver letter slot, the hatstand, the creaking
   stairs, their own bedroom looking out to a small patch of garden ...

The children in bed, the lopsided gate still lopsided, the call
of night in fading light, a last check on the roses on the wall,

and again she waits for him. On the back porch lighting coals,
she can breathe now. She moves the hookah. Whatever wall

she had ever come against is not here. Here I am learning
to say *um-ber-ella*, trying on loose laughter inside a wall

of things I cannot forget. Here I can take what he's given
me, can weed, my headscarf in the rhododendrons. Wall

of my English garden, mine. My husband, mine. He plants
Sally Mac, Red Devil, a floribunda and a tea, near the wall,

then cuts them and puts them in a vase on the windowsill.
Here I'm not *the crime of my geography*, I am Salwa, a wall

walling in something like hope. This father to the fragrance
of the flower I will go with forever. His work is his, his wall

his; mine, mine. We will return to the planet's oldest city.
We'll carry in us lopsided gates and yellow roses on a wall.

INTIMATE DAWN, acrylic on canvas, 52.25" x 40" MMXXI

TO LET THEM GO

On the third day, Tarek took the songbirds back out to the
hillside to let them go, unbanded, amid the apricot trees.

Tarek was fourteen. He was a bird catcher at Beit Jala. He didn't know
what he'd found in the mist net, and he didn't know he'd let them go

either. He'd never seen such beauteous mystery in a bird, weighing
hardly more than the band he was to band them with. He would go

home first to be with them for a while, feed them, love the green
in their jeweled heads, find out what they were first. Then he'd go

on with his job, perhaps, of writing down wing length, tail size, sex,
weight, percentage of body fat. Mitterrand ordered his chef to go

and find these birds for his last meal. Tarek had no way of knowing
that. He also didn't know what deep inside him told him not to go

on with what he'd been told was his job. He placed the two bands
with his two birds' serial numbers onto a silver chain. He would go

still with his brothers and his friends to sling stones. It would not
change everything in him, but every day he decided he had to go

on with what was expected of him, those two ortolan buntings
went with him. They didn't free him, but they didn't let him go.

THE USUAL SURPRISE, acrylic on paper, 15" x 20" MMXVIII

MONA HARDIN

A frigatebird can stay aloft for two whole months
without touching down on either land or water.

We know a lot about living in flyways, flying over town after town
after town for weeks over land and water without touching down,

sleeping in air drafts, getting food however we get food, taking it
as we have to take it, until one night one of our own is taken down.

"Officer, I'm scared. I'm your brother. I'm scared." *That's my son.*
"I beat the ever-living fuck out of him, choked him" comes down

to us months later when we hear Officer Hollingsworth's rage,
see him, Ronald Greene, beaten, shackled, dragged, face down

on the asphalt on a highway near Monroe. We hear something
like "I hope the fucker didn't have AIDS." He is pushed down

again when he tries to roll on his side so he can breathe. This
goes on for 9 minutes before he goes limp, finally goes down

for the last time. We are told he died in a car accident, a high
speed chase involved. We live with that lie for months. Down

in the Delta we see monarchs, swans, songbirds. I've never seen
a frigatebird but I know something of its annihilating drop down.

WE ARE, acrylic on canvas, 14" x 11" MMXX

OBJECT LESSON

And if they were ever anything other than objects, they
were objects to be feared, because, if you didn't fear them
then they would become real people. And we didn't want
them to be real people, we couldn't handle that.

When a soldier yells at you to *lift your fucking shirt*, he doesn't hear
himself or soundings in a stone-on-stone wall he's making of his fear.

When the other soldiers tell you to drop your remaining underwear,
to stand over a mirror and squat, you know you are incarcerated fear

turned over and trapped inside someone else. You, a reconfigured
unperson, force, sign, belief, ideology, enmity. You, a network fear

has construed to erase who you are. You are not yet the father of
the girl they will kill, just a gimp with a limp, and gimps work fear

to their advantage. The limp is just the beginning of who they are.
The soldiers know that much. Whatever it is you pray to they fear,

the cave you lived in as a child, they fear. Your learning Hebrew,
your love of Rumi and Darwish, your stay in London, they fear.

Your study, your love of gardens filled with oranges, your roses
climbing your walls, your marriage and your children, they fear.

Your brotherhood with men and women so exactly like you. Hope
threaded into grief. Memory. What makes you human, they fear.

LESSON 3: BEING HERE, acrylic on canvas, 46" x 67" MMXX

FOG

The hills of Jerusalem are a bath of fog ...
Geography here is everything.

Even the unaided human ear hears it, the muffle in the ring,
the muted horn, the audiology of grief, and how everything

is never as it has been. The news comes at you in your car,
you recognize the street or the district where everything's

been taken down for blocks, or where they have strangled
someone for selling illegal cigarettes. You've lost everything

that was ever yours. Your wife is there with you. You swim
toward the shadow she is on some other side. Everything

is shrouded. Jerusalem could be Birmingham in Alabama.
Four little girls in a church are erased again as is everything

they could have been if they were not crimes of their own
geography. Addie Mae, hate-filled dust all over everything,

Cynthia, Carole, Abir, Carol Denise. Smadar, this Sorority
of Innocents we are called to bury. Bombs are everything

to terrorists everywhere. The rubber bullet that killed Abir,
soldiers call a Lazarus pill. But terror blurs. Levels everything.

FROM A DISTANCE, acrylic on canvas, 24" x 18" MMXX

ANNUNCIATION

It seemed the sort of place where he could have grown up.
He wanted to whisper to it, to announce his recognition.

I am in the Musée d'Orsay standing before the famous Whistler
there, the one opposite *A Burial at Ornans*, hearing this whisper

about the geometry I am standing in, me talking to myself again.
The grave behind me, its attendants, a dog, the thurible whisper

back, sound as soft as the smoke that caught in the boy's throat
when the censer had been lighted once. *I've been here* I whisper

to no one but to this place or to these places where everything
is not as it was before. The way that little painting is a whisper

of a landscape, or industrial cityscape, in the room before me
now does not seem to matter. What matters is how a whisper

matters in this place I've finally come to, how a thing impossible
before now is possible and happening in me, how this whisper

is as mystical as anything that ever moved in any mystic mind.
I know the woman in the chair, the foot stool, the lacy whisper

in the whites, the folded hands, the patience, the quiet repose,
and how essential that drape is where vine and flowers whisper.

A NOTE FROM THE WATERSIDE, acrylic on canvas, 3o" x 24" MMXVIII

ONE MORE RIVER TO CROSS

It is often a surprise to travelers that the River Jordan is,
in so many places, not much more than a trickle.

It's hayfields and horses and bean fields and sugar cane, and rice ponds
turned to crawfish ponds in off season all around us. Not a river in sight.

But the river in song is never a river as the river in story is never just river.
We sing "Jordan River" here holding each other in more than sight

lines. That *one more river to cross* is more than getting to the other side
of anything you might think of as other side. The other side is new sight

we see only in the stories we have to tell. Smadar and Abir are here,
violent river stories now. Rami and Nurit grieve here. Said right, sight

makes a Floyd, a Baldwin, a Medgar, a King. Bassam and Salwa love here.
We hardly ever think of river breadth or width here, we never lose sight

of what we have to cross, or how we cross, or who we'll cross it with.
There's ever singing in the waters, a holding on to everything in sight.

The blood trickling down from Amédé was not the color of his skin,
the same wine-dark red as the blood of his assailants. No oversight

by no account. It will not be over until we talk. We cannot choke all
the stories out of all the people. Darnella Frazier has us in her sight.

SIX VISITORS, acrylic on canvas, 46" x 70" MMXVIII

ARABESQUES AND DIAGONALS

But there were times he would look back through the sketchbooks,
searching for ideas, and be taken by the patterns themselves, their
ragged sense of purpose, their forms growing out of necessity.

The way she tilted slightly off-center and did those few last turns
in the dance, barely suggesting flourish. Those were the patterns

that came to him when he told the stories, wrote the ads, drew
the sketches. He could lose himself in pictures of the patterns

in the Mosque-Cathedral of Córdoba and in all the dancing tiles
coming at him as he approached the Dome. Memory patterns

life for him that way. In the dance class she was going to take
she moves along diagonals. It's jazz after all. His story patterns

itself. Each time he tells it he is surprised by the persistence of
the echo of ragged purpose. If the bombings were not patterns

and this loss were unprecedented lunacy, it still would be loss
immeasurable and ragged still. He knows blindness patterns

blindness. Hate patterns hate. Power patterns power. But grief
and hope do too. Children dancing or people talking patterns

a way to be. In the old days a widow wanting to marry again
wove a red thread in her hem knowing the power in patterns.

MEMORY GARDEN, acrylic on canvas, 24" x 3o" MMXVII

STANDING UP TO IT

The women met each Sunday at the Santa Rita de Casia church in Havana,
    with photographs of their jailed loved ones pinned to their chests.

Anna Akhmatova went to Leningrad Prison each day to stand. To be broken in half
is not the poet's worst fate. First lines often begin there. She carried a photograph

of her disappeared son in her purse. To be beloved poet of the nation did not quell
the *one hundred million voices* shouting inside her *tortured mouth*. The photograph

of the broken spirit does not exist but the broken spirit surely does. Izzat Ghazzawi
taught. *Forgive us our longing if it intensifies* he wrote. No one took a photograph

of him being strip-searched several mornings a week in front of his students, him
making his way to Birzeit to teach them. At Atara checkpoint, who can photograph

is tightly controlled and none of the control is given to any Palestinian on site.
The intention of the search sears far more than whatever forbidden photograph

anyone might dare to take. Las Damas de Blanco gathered for lawyers, students,
journalists, intellectuals imprisoned for free thought. Each woman's photograph

is pinned near her heart. They won the European Parliament Sakharov Prize.
Laura Pollán, Berta Solar, Miriam Leiva, Loida Valdes, Julia Núnëz, no photograph

of any of the leaders invited to accept it. Their government barred their travel.
Nurit asked for no applause when she won it. In her purse, Smadar's photograph.

LIONHEART, acrylic on canvas, 36" x 24" MMXXI

PILGRIMAGE

Don't get me wrong, he said. We will never give up.
It is not our intention to walk away.

The meeting rooms of the lawmakers are filled with talk
of what to do with us while we whisper how we'll walk

& where & with what constraints & with what defiance.
In Paris or Myanmar or Minneapolis, we will not walk

away from our death & dying, or from who we are.
They burned our homes in Cadie. They made us walk

from our settlements & our tribal villages. They put us
in collars, padlocks, chains, ropes. If we'd ever walk

again after long sea voyages, they gave but scant
thought to. The haunted dreams where the walk

back toward the smell of our mothers' cooking was
the dream of missing all the right turns. The walk

in lines for food in camps, how so many fell in line,
how the fallen were dragged away, how the walk

never ended even if we did not move. Occupiers
& slavers know nothing of how or where we walk.

WATER FOR TIME, acrylic on canvas, 53" x 80" MMXIX

THE WATERY SADNESS THAT NEVER GOES AWAY

Did you water the petunias?

Countably infinite are the ways grief will quarter
us. The same is true of rage, and of love. Water

fills the ponds and lakes and marshes for birds
that will come to us in the flyovers. I love water

coming in slanting sheets, the storms that clean
the air. I live with this persistent *did you water*

the petunias in my head. In urns near doorways
petunias are wilting. In the wilt is need of water

we must be mindful to bring to them. My friend
in his evening hours in his garden carries water

to his roses and Clementines and Chinese oranges.
They are his lights in darker times, he says. Water

and petunias, and migrating pelicans and grebes,
stork-filled ponds and those sweet dancing water

birds skittering here and there, and grief finding
its place in me again, diving in me like I'm water.

THE DEEP HOURS, acrylic on canvas, 48" x 60" MMXXI

IZZAT AL-GHAZZAWI OPENS THE PAGE OF ABSENCE

Do not let the olive branch fall from my hands.

Who would not remember exactly where they were when the call
came? In dreams I cannot wake up from, I am there. I see him fall.

He was 16, the snipers above the school yard picked him from all
the rest. We hold olive branches still, Arafat and me. We will fall

if branches fall, even here. We cannot be lost forever with martyrs
who were our sons, our daughters, our brothers, our sisters. Fall,

you might think is the hardest time of the year for those above
and below, as we. Darwish is spreading colorful nets for the fall

of olives from the trees. Cranes and pelicans darken the skies
this time of year, along with the other birds. Some birds fall

like leaves fall, like sons fall, so many children marking indelible
traces on who we are, wherever we are. Even if our speeches fall

on deaf ears, you will not erase us. Let's be clear about that one
thing. If Palestinians did not exist in 1948, wherever did they fall

to when the whole country was *disappeared*? What treaty says
a next step is to expunge remainders or whatever does not fall?

ACCORDING TO WHAT, acrylic on canvas, 60" x 42" MMXX

THE BUMPER STICKER

It will not be over until we talk.

All our prayers and dreams about crossing over, so we walk
over to the crossing-over place. At the checkpoints the talk

is talk we cannot understand. They walked us out like cattle
from our lands in Tennessee, Florida, Alabama, the sky over

us like the sky we had always known. The world we walked
toward was not going to be the not-world. Our stories talk

to us in ways others do not understand. We told the stories
but we had to be quieter in the telling. We told them over

campfires, in sickness, hungry, beaten, drunken, face down
in dirt. We know of life partitioned where people do not talk.

Children die there as others write treatises and draw maps
of holy lands and promised lands. Passage is not a cross over

as cross over could be. No, it's all rights and ownership and
occupation and sacred spaces and forbidden places, and talk

is talk of war. Oh, bracelet of children, Goodchild, Ibrahim, Uri,
Zaahir, Naomi, Dakota, Aliyah, Winona, Tamir's life here is over.

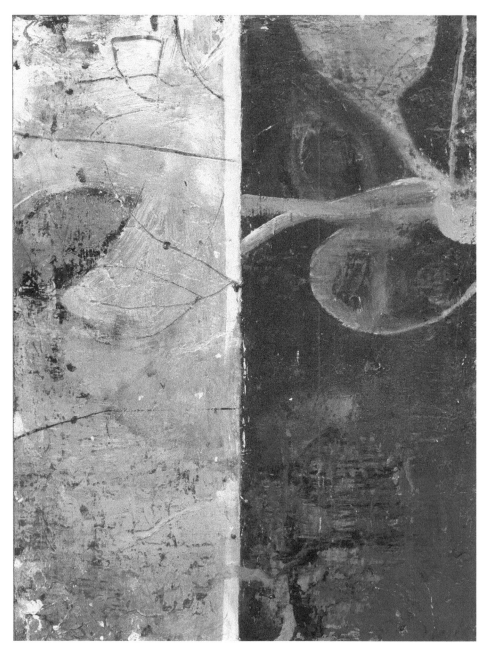

I AND I, acrylic and graphite on canvas, 26" x 20" MMXX

SURVIVAL

... [Edward Said] the Palestinian critic wrote: *Survival, in fact, is about the connections between things*. It was one of Nurit's favorite books ...

We build walls around all those things we want to remain unseen.
What we are & what we are not, it all happens in the in between.

Entre, nel mezzo, idir, zwischen, yn y canol. In Mandarin, Hebrew,
Yiddish, Urdu, Korean, hardly a language is without an in between.

Mājhē in Bengali is the word, better represented in its own alphabet.
Before East Pakistan was Bangladesh, India was the vast in between

separating it from another Pakistan. The West Bank & Gaza Strip
make what we know today of Palestine, & Israel is its in between,

building walls & checkpoints where strip-searching is a security
measure. Consider this one act for starters. There is no in between

built for survival built on blood & bombs & rubber bullets & fear
& denial & blindness. Said maps out cartographies of in between

where humans can see human, where law holds itself together
with philharmonics over power inside our common in between.

Edward Said travels with the mind of winter. His work declines
exile, conjugates how we breathe in the geography of in between.

DAYBREAK, acrylic on canvas, 3o" X 24" MMXVII

1 OF 1001 PATHS TO THE MONASTERY AT BEIT JALA

Among scholars of Islam, mathematical numbers are
considered to be not just quantities, but qualities too.

Whether the tea is served in fancy bowls or in what looks like tumblers
from the West, whether in a souk or in a diner, it matters. So numbers

matter too in ways we often overlook. The boy was 6 when his father
took him to Jerusalem told him and his brothers 3 stories: the numbers

Muhammad left with others as he traveled on his night flight, the gold
melted for the roof of the Dome, one story of the designs of numbers

in the minds of guildsmen making the minbar of Saladin. This boy in
prison knows what happens on which day in a hunger strike, numbers

of blows or kicks when he is beaten or is forced to beat his cell mates,
remembers the day of the month he found King and Gandhi, numbers

of deaths in those men's stories too, how they corresponded to the life
he was living then and would live until 2005. And then after. Numbers

of nights alone he studied the Holocaust in a library in England. Nights
in Jericho are dark until he sees the gold of the Dome in the numbers

of oranges hanging from branches in his garden and he finds himself
in flight to a settlement of unknowns, an algebra of healing numbers.

WHAT LIGHT THERE IS, acrylic on canvas, 42" x 3o" MMXX

GRIEF'S GEOMETRY

To be bereaved in Israel is to be part of a tradition,
something really terrible but holy at the same time.

Pauline Opango Lamumba still walks the streets of Leopold City, aggrieved
and bare-breasted, demanding the body of her husband. A wife bereaved

followed by the press will live as long as photography lives. Thin dark veils
over gutted grief, Jackie, Coretta, Ethel and Betty shadowed the bereaved

of whole nations. Veils of nakedness echo grief in towers. You can hear it
in some calls to prayer from minarets, from minbars and pulpits bereaved

of their guides. The world is full, brimmed with mourning mothers, brothers
sisters, fathers who do not know how to live in their own houses, bereaved

of daughters dancing or buying candy bracelets. I think of Lincoln holding
lifeless Willie's body as everything was breaking all around him, bereaved

and holding inside some terrible geometrics he will not live long enough
to fathom. I think of Myrlie, the children in residential schools bereaved

of everything they knew, parents, language, fry bread. I think of Gianna
Floyd, I think of Diamond Reynolds' little daughter who knew bereaved

before Philando Castile was shot. It was the terror in her mother's voice
brought her to the holy moment. Four-year olds should not be bereaved.

THIS, acrylic on canvas, 24" x 3o" MMXVI

SHE WAS TEN

and when he said it he slid the photograph of Abir across the
table, a large glossy, eight by ten, *You murdered my daughter*, and the
Senator wasn't even ruffled, he picked up the photo, nodded, laid it
down carefully ... He knew exactly what Bassam meant, he said.

Imagine Shostakovich or Akhmatova being muzzled or muffled.
They would have suffocated. Her poems refused to be ruffled,

his Seventh Symphony unfolded as it had to. *I wanted to convey
the context of grim events*, he says. He put aside those ruffled

sounds, put aside the crash of battle. A madman had set his sight
on starving their beloved Leningrad to death. What was ruffled

in them would have to wait. We live the stories when everything
is flying everywhere, but we tell them when we have unruffled

the terrors and something like a god in us calms those waters
we might have drowned in. Imagine this father, how ruffled

still he was by who he was. Imagine him carrying the photograph
with him, imagine him holding it flying over. Imagine the ruffled

heart of the Senator who had to hold what he knew to be true
within him in this moment. This is tightwire walking, a ruffled

everything held by the thread that keeps us steady on the wire
so we can tell the story face to face, and hear it told, unruffled.

47

WHAT I CAN SEE FROM HERE, acrylic on canvas, 48″ x 64″ MMXVII

3 O'CLOCK IN THE AFTERNOON

On and on and on this went, month after month, year after year,
until the fourth of September, 1997, just a few days before Yom Kipper,
when this incredible bubble burst in midair into a million
pieces.

On   pieces
and   midair

on   burst
and   bubble

on   incredible
              before

                   days
                                                    few

1997
September

                                             fourth
year   after   year

                   after   year
month   after

pieces   after
              million   pieces

JUST BEYOND THIS PLACE, acrylic on paper, 10" x 15.75" MMXVI

THIS FAMILY

This is how our two families met. We were meeting
as enemies who now wanted to speak.

Something happened. I was no longer inside your homily.
I was living inside this new thing I came to call *this family*.

The Dome of the Rock, the first day of Ramadan 2021,
courts, evictions, rockets, death-rains on this family.

The arborist tells me ancestors planted this oak tree
in my back yard. It is my ancestor I say — of this family.

Trees are beings, I tell the arborist, and crows and forests,
and nightingales near garden walls singing for this family.

How much time has to pass before we come to name
all the beings we try to keep from being in this family.

Auditoriums fill with people. These people come to hear
their stories filled with the fallen children of this family.

We are trying to find a way. *It won't stop until we talk.*
The endless passing of time we call grief in this family.

Je suis Bassam Aramin, et Salwa, Rami Elhanan, et Nurit,
les parents d'Abir et Smadar. You cannot erase this family.

They bulldozed the ancient olive groves to punish us,
not knowing the time it takes a tree to die in this family.

9 A. M., acrylic on canvas, 32" x 24" MMXX

EARLY IN THE MORNING

But on January 16, 2007 — two years after Combatants for Peace was founded — my ten-year-old daughter, Abir, walked out from her school ... She was just by the school gates when she was shot by a member of the Israeli border police. With a rubber bullet. An American-made M-16. From an American-made jeep ... She had just bought herself some candy.

from her
border

shot by
police

M-16
American-made

Jeep
American-made

rubber bullet
ten-year-old

Israeli border ...
some candy

walked out from her school
... for Peace

shot early in the morning
January 16, 2007

SHE DOESN'T TELL ME HOW, acrylic on canvas, 16" x 12" MMXXI

SHE TOLD ME ONCE

She told me once she wanted to be an engineer. Can you
imagine what sort of bridges she could have built?

You must have the mind of winter the old poet says. You've left ridges
there of who you were. You're like snow in a world with its own bridges.

You live away, mostly. The rubber bullet, the exile, the erasure, the boy
in the vehicle doing what he was told to do, the checkpoints, all bridges

to the scattered girl on the floor next to her sister's bed, the girl learning
maths or buying candy bracelets. The bracelet was one of the bridges

I kept with me. It almost brought me more Occupation than I already
had. I am the man you called father. When they excavate your bridges,

they will find me. I am the man you called father. I'll keep saying that.
I will learn more new languages. I will go wherever your story bridges

you to who we are. I find you in Belfast, in a senator's heart. You rise
for us like the spirits in those mystics whirling inside those bridges

they whirl themselves into before they come down again by being
who they are. They love the world with them in it, and those bridges

and flyovers of prayer, and everything that has ever lived still leaving
its mark. *Ask Rumi*, ask Said, *ask Stevens. Ask any builder of bridges*.

REQUIEM, acrylic on paper, 14.5" x 23" MMXVI

I CAN'T BREATHE

The rim of a tightening lung.

The naming endless. It knows no geography, no skin color, no
caste. Tamir, Breonna, Abir, Barrabas, Sadat, Smadar. A lung

filled with air is pink and light. As light as a candy bracelet or
birds' bones, or truce so tenuous you hold your breath. A lung

might hold the idea of peace the way Picasso's dove might hold
an olive branch, a flower, or some honey-sweetened other lung

making its way finally toward the beloved in the same flyway as
strangled words. *Eloi, Eloi* or *Mama, Mama,* the range of a lung

holding diminished air in the last moment, endless. Philandro,
Trayvon, Eric, Sandra, Martin, Janisha, Malcolm, Dante's lung.

He could feel it more and more in the last moments, him hung
there, naked, nailed, thirsting, and the rim of a tightening lung.

Collapsed and punctured, Ronald Greene, Trayford Pellerin,
Freddie Gray, Emmet Till, Alton Sterling. One shuttered lung,

then another. Myrlie Evers at her doorstep, her three children
shouting, "Daddy, get up!" One shot, more than one empty lung.

RUMOURS OF AN EXIT, acrylic on canvas, 30" x 40" MMXVII

THE JERICHO HOUSE

The architecture of well-appointed houses in Jericho is such
that they are considered introverted —   many of their
rooms point their gaze towards the inner courtyard rather
than out into the street: they gather into themselves.

Everything gets blown apart, and we cannot see the inner structure
or any part of where we lived before. The remaining architecture

is no consolation. We live now in an inner courtyard with herb
patches here and there. How leaves make roofs is architecture.

Look at the spires from bulbs of green onions. Mint is not a street
form. Some stubborn onions do end up in street life. Architecture

of mind is something Voltaire knew all about. We cannot impede
the grand march of terror or the absurd, and gaze in architecture

is where it settles us. Us looking inward is not a denial of having to
look outward too. A building can help us to know the architecture

of who we are. In this new house my wife touched the walls. She
moved in the house, touched everything, a braille the architecture

opened for her here. I saw her. She wiped the dampness from her
cheeks. Nothing of the past is ever changed but this architecture

brought us closer to the houses we have become, a house within
another house. We are not apologizing for the house's architecture.

HARD RAIN, acrylic on canvas, 36" x 48" MMXV

LONG AND FREQUENT SHOWERS

And we think the myths are startling.

Apollo killed her sons and Aphrodite her daughters. Niobe's tears
we know because we know the myth. Myths take years on years

to shape themselves. Salwa's tears are another thing, or the Israeli
mother, halfway through her morning run. Her son of eleven years

gone out for bread or to play hacky sack with friends. *Il a disparu*
the French would say. This feels like a myth she might say if years

could give her back her tongue. *La Llorona* has cousins all over
the world. She's Cihuacōātl, she's Eve. Hebrew, Aztec. For years

after the bombing Rami took long showers so Nurit would not hear
him sobbing. In tears he knows his kin. She's Lamia, Lilith. The years

the Palestinian woman carried the photograph of her fallen child,
she wanted all to see what she could not cipher. Grief lives years

past a half-life. Being and not being live in the same house all too
often. A wandering mother wolf tracks the same tracks for years.

A mother crow is flying through the copse she flew toward to feed
her own. Grief is countably infinite but never counts itself in years.

THE NOW THAT WAS, acrylic on canvas, 42" x 30" MMXX

CALL FROM NETANYAHU

Not now, not for shiva, no, please do not show your face. She put the
phone down, then tipped the receiver over so it was off the hook.

What madness comes to you on that morning you could never
have prepared yourself for, the morning you are the receiver

of the calls and this one comes. Always strong-willed, a Bibi
in the fever of his making, strong-willed, always the receiver,

even in this swirling-in-power request of his. You're trying
to learn to breathe again in this blur of time as a receiver

is listening to everything you have to say this morning after
the bombing. You're a sketch figure making you the receiver

of the ways you fit into the script they hold on to. Rami
is, as ever, near. Elik, Guy, little Yigar holding on. Receiver

each of this thing they had never been before, never held
before in hand or heart or head. We become the receiver

of some new label we cannot wrap our being around. One day
before we were all survivors-at-large. Today, each a receiver

of who or what? Grief does not come in the order they say it
will. I am Peled-Elhanan. I will not be the silence in the receiver.

AERIAL BOUNDARIES, acrylic on canvas, 3o" x 24" MMXX

MY SISTER SCISSORING THE AIR ABOVE US

Abir's sister, Areen, was in the habit of scissoring out the
newspaper clippings ... Sometimes at night, when she couldn't
sleep, she'd reach in under the bed for the box, and wake in
the morning with her sister scattered all around her.

The frigate birds fly high and long. We see them as flickering
above us if we see them at all. They don't rely on scissoring

the way other birds do. They can stay up in the air for weeks.
It's said they sleep in clouds and there, there is no scissoring.

It's all release and ease and ride. But even frigate birds must
eat. The fall for food nearly shatters them. They, scissoring

their way out of stupor, meet need. Memory comes that way
at us, and grief as well. We're tied to ribboned tags scissoring

their way toward us. We have the implement in hand before
we even know we are cutting and pasting this life, scissoring

past our efforts at letting go. The Buddhists are right, of course,
about letting go, but how are we, we ask, to go about scissoring

away a sister taken into flight in someone else's war. She was
buying a candy bracelet when a boy sent the bullet scissoring

its way to her from behind. My father sits in the playground
with his friend. They're falling from clouds. They're scissoring.

IN TOUCH WITH THE GROUND, acrylic on canvas, 48" x 36" MMXXI

PLANTATION/RESERVATION/
TERRITORY/SETTLEMENT

> The roads they had taken, the turns, the roundabouts, the
> red signs. They had different names for the areas they had
> traveled through, varying pronunciations of streets.

No one comes here untouched. Whether it's the scarring burns
of love or lust, accident or arrangement, we all have our turns

at this passing we call a life and we are all indigenous peoples,
born in a somewhere where others are not born. What turns

over in us is land we take and call ours. *Our* home. *Our* nation.
That's the shift that sticks, adjusts topographies, blocks turns

at checkpoints. We direct passage because we can. We invent
language and infrastructures. Reservation is how *stolen* turns

to *gift*, to *allowance*. Settlements are reasoned right and just,
not appropriation built on power or on fear, right? What turns

out for us is good and you're just *shit outta luck* if you're not
us. You're Romany? Keep traveling and tinkering, Your turns

toward genius in a Django Reinhardt, an anomaly. Your father,
your grandmother, her mother, your olive trees, nothing turns

you into what we do not want to see. One drop or pure bred,
none of it matters. Occupation is not a game of taking turns.

THE FAR END OF THE GARDEN, acrylic on canvas, 32" x 24" MMXX

HADIQA

You can hate me all you want, that is fine. You can build all
the walls you want, that is fine. If you think a wall gives you
security go ahead, but make it in your garden, not mine.

It is "the turk," not Candide, who first says *Il faut cultiver notre jardin.*
Voltaire was easy to enrage. How important to Muslims the garden

is was his way of rapping Enlightenment knuckles. It was not science,
or love, or reason would keep us safe from power or fear. A garden

is not the outside world we have to go into. He had no illusions about
that, or the dangers there. He knew the exile for speaking the garden

tongue of his true mind. Voltaire does not tell us of Chateau de Cirey
or how he got it, or of Madame de Châtelet, or what kind of a garden

they tended there. That was for another book, stories that took him
more than three days to write. His one true thinker in this garden

of a song, "the turk," knows the power of tyrants and what a shape-
shifter power is. He knows fear too. A small fig orchard is a garden

he seems to say, so is a bed for carrots, herbs, cucumbers. The rug
with the four rivers flowing into the navel of the world is a garden.

The world without a place for grace or goodness is not a place to live.
Watering Clementines is part of the maths of "the turk" in his garden.

FOR SEVERAL MOMENTS, acrylic on canvas, 42" x 3o" MMXXI

NO NAILS, NO GLUE

… the secret to the structure was that the thousands of parts were
not hung on a framework at all, but were harmoniously integrated.

The secret of mystery hangs inside us, unfabricated
for centuries until the burning asks to be integrated

into what is not burning. In Einstein's life of queries,
he asks if peace will have a place on that integrated

tremble near the fulcrum on the scale. Old physicist,
who seems like he was ever old, sought an integrated

universe. He heard something like a god in his violin,
a god in the Unknown in maths, numbers integrated

in a world without glue or nails. Nothing mattered so
much as what mattered. But nothing gets integrated

in fires of zealots or bombs, choke holds or unswerving
certainty. Michael Brown falling, or Trayvon integrated

finally with the bullet Zimmerman delivered that night
in Florida. One man sees himself recorded, integrated

to nothing. It's all glue and nails again … no breathing.
In stories of race or caste or class nothing is integrated.

DESIRE, acrylic on canvas, 6o" x 4o" MMXIX

SINÉAD O'CONNOR SINGS *ALIYAH*

The plastic tape rollers were melted and jammed
on the song *Nothing Compares 2 U.*

There are those songs that never leave us, those rising songs
coming at us like rockets in dreams, all our past lives melted

on the spot in their passing through us. Young girls bruise
their knees dancing into things until they have melted

inside, young boys too are not immune. *It's been so lonely
without you here / Like a bird without a song.* The melted

heart knows no particular geography, no Israel here, no
Ireland, no Palestine, Muslim-Jew-Arab, all labels melted

away by saints and troubadours. No Prince, no anti-Prince,
just a U mattering more than anything. Tekakwitha melted

too inside things she heard that others did not. Her native
name *bumps into things* says it all. Her holy blues melted

things we can hardly know, but *All the flowers that you
planted, mother / in the backyard, / All died* has melted

more than just young hearts in troubled lands. And … *when
you went away* calls us. Walls fall there, all partition melted.

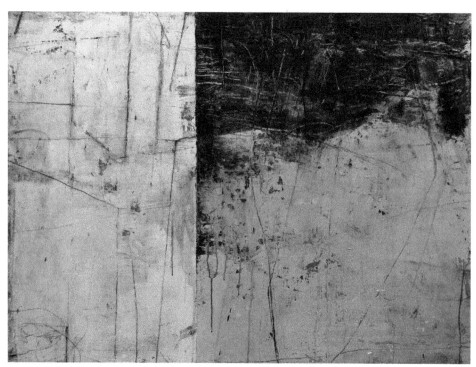

THE OUTGOING TIDE, acrylic and graphite on canvas, 3o" x 4o.5" MMXIX

THE NEWLY ARRIVED

> It is a tradition in both Israel and Palestine ... to give gifts
> of fresh bread and sea salt to newly arrived strangers.

It's easy to forget the kindnesses we have in common, how to gently be
with each other. The Natives may have never seen the reconfigured sea

right before their eyes, ships coming to them or at them as it turned out
to be. Who knows if they did not go for bread or salt, or fishes of the sea,

or whatever gifts they gave to strangers when they were trying to figure
out what this new thing was coming over the horizon. They knew the sea

of the ancestors, something mostly good to them, a something as familiar
as the lapping of aunts, uncles, shamans and spirit peoples inside the sea

they called their lives on this edge of everything they could not know. No
guns yet, fire water, no blankets yet, no talk in languages filled with a sea

of sounds neither could hear. What to make of strange garbled words like
reservation, settlement. In a time before navigational aids, to be *all at sea*

was to be in danger, to lose sight of land as we lose sight of land today. And
Smadar dies. Parents must not die in allotted lands or partitions by the sea.

Abir, King, Sadat, Chief Joseph are all among the dead. Occupation hates
a stranger. It has no gift to give, no bread or tobacco, no salt from any sea.

EMPYREAL, acrylic on canvas, 32" x 24" MMXX

BORGES IN JERUSALEM

Jorge Luis Borges, when walking with guides through Jerusalem in
the early 70s, said he had never seen a city of such clear searing light.

He liked walking in the Palestinian neighborhoods, hearing
the quiet passages of ghosts in alleyways, smelling searing

meats on the kababs over fires in souks. He made something
of family there with the sighted of heart and mind. Searing

light was one other thing he could see, he said. The stones
of Jerusalem were pink as he was once before the searing

sun of his homeland and his bloodlines turned him brown
as his brothers here. Absence in lovers' hearts turn searing

to seeing, and seeing stone clarifies seeing a thousandfold
at least. I want to be near you with this clear light searing

all of us into being whoever it is we can be when we see as
beloveds were always meant to see. Let me be this searing

for you. I am saying *Being with you, and not being with you,*
is the only way I have to measure time. Each of us searing

in our griefs, each of us scrambled in each other's stories.
To be me in a broken holy land. Oh, holy, blessed searing.

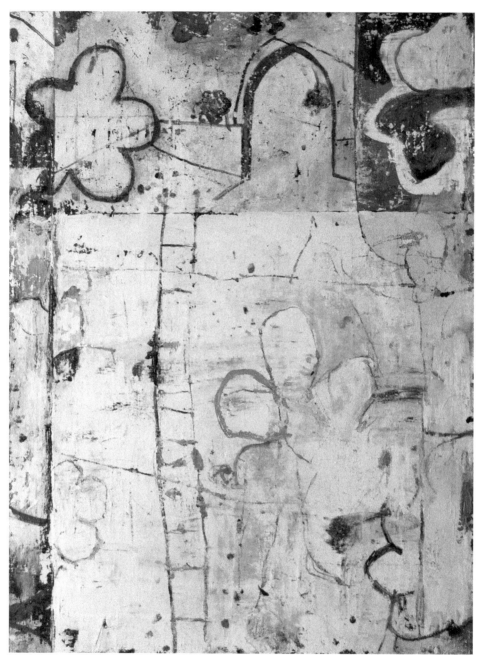

THE SAME STORY, acrylic on canvas, 40" x 30" MMXVIII

STORY

One story becoming another.

In that time when he wasn't fully awake he'd hear the sound of the lorry braking, then he'd remember he was back in Jericho. He'd been one story

for so long. That's the way a childhood works. He was the son who didn't get the vaccine, so he was the son with the limp. That held as his story

through the years. He grew up in a cave near Hebron until Israeli forces evicted the family. He was a stone slinger like other boys, each a story

in his own right. At 17 he was imprisoned. He went on a 17 day hunger strike. He was released after 7 years. He often couldn't believe his story

was his story. He met a Jewish guard in prison, took classes in Hebrew, began his Holocaust studies. He married and had 6 children, one story

after another story in each of the children. When she was 10 his daughter was killed by a rubber bullet to the back of the head. Hers was the story

he would tell until his last day. He left his homeland to get his degree in the history of the people history cut him off from, figures in a story

he would come to see himself in. He tended walled gardens. He ended his evenings there with his beloved. She is his story in a story in a story.

THE PAST BEFORE US, acrylic on canvas, 60" x 40" MMXXI

MAY DAY, MAY DAY, MAY DAY

> ... *mayday* ... derived from the French *venez m'aider* ...
> is always repeated three times ... The repetition is vital.

You call and it is your true brother who will see the sign
in the sound of your voice coming through on the line,

will pick up the hoe or the shovel as the mourners lean
over the grave, will shovel the first dirt, will find a line

from just the right poem to read in the moment you go
to the other place you have to go to. There's a fine line

between actual death and all those other little deaths
that come in a life: loss of a child, the break in a line

of swans, swan coming at you as you fly a mission you
gave your word to, the crumbling of hope, a long line

of voters waiting to vote in a nation hell–bent on not
giving each voter a voice, the last tree falling in a line

of trees falling in rain forests. Death as a countably
infinite number of sides. Like life, or love. Like a line

coming from who knows where. We hear metal rollers.
Me, Nurit, Smadar, all of us in pieces, all a broken line.

OVERCAST, acrylic on canvas, 42" x 30" MMXX

A ONE-CIGARETTE GARDEN

He moves along the wall to the second tree, fills the well of it, and
then tightens the nozzle, stops the flow of water, steps towards the
clementines and the Chinese orange trees, their small bursts of color.

In the other garden, the one in England, he'd hear the lark's song,
children laughing, big grown men cheering sports teams. One long

deep breath was more possible there than anywhere he'd been
before. Tonight sharp pain he's lived with all his life returns along

with all this quiet, this dark dark, and the cigarettes he must give up
another time. They ease the pain it seems. A scarf of smoke as long

as the one waving to him from his daughter's neck rises above him.
She runs down the street from him to meet her friends. How long

has it been, how long will it be, will it become something else, ever?
Water is scarce here. He pulls the yellow hose behind him. One long

pull on the cigarette behind his ear might help. He decides against it,
snaps the hose behind him every few feet. First the citrus trees along

the wall, then the vegetables, then the loofah vines. Little trenches
he's made hold the precious water, little wells making lines as long

as little rivers drunk by darkened earth. Flowers on the Clementines
and Chinese orange trees. He and the oranges, they're coming along.

EDEN PLAY, acrylic on canvas, 40" x 60" MMXIX

CONVENTION

... it is not a decree of faith that we should live forever
with a sword in our hands. I cannot tell you what sort of
madness it seemed. And I was completely cleaved open.

See the birds in flyovers. Breakaway is double edged. We believed,
as the good children we wanted to be, in a golden silence, cleaved

to patterns and designs that were ours, they said. You will learn
to breathe, they said. It was history, family, the glue they cleaved

to, and we were to do the same. Culture, tradition, the march of
history tells us who we are. Ignore Papal Bulls. What is cleaved

to you will tell you who you are. They kept saying that. Ignore
Trails of Tears, stick to your own kind and you will be cleaved

to your own kind. Ignore what does not look like you, they say.
Do not go beyond your father's saying or you will be cleaved

open and on your own. But to go beyond decrees, to fall in love
with an arc other than the sword's arc, just might have us cleaved

to that arc of justice the peace-maker talked of in his sermons,
to that arc of physics, that arc of goodness, to what this *cleaved*

has always meant. One word can mean two things or more.
Why not us? Why not talk? Why not a congress of the cleaved?

CINNABAR, acrylic on canvas, 42" x 3o" MMXXI

LIFTING WEIGHT

What are you going to do now with this new,
unbearable burden on your shoulders?

You can hardly remember what it was like when these boulders
were not yours to carry. You'd brag about the strong shoulders

that came with your stock. You had been a warrior, you'd kept
yourself in shape after, you'd carried children on your shoulders

through the streets and into the countryside. You'd been here
for generations. You knew the mess of history, how it shoulders

itself into the traces of the grand march, how little it cares about
what you cared about or who you cared for or how a shoulder's

blade might be our body's yoke to birds if we are poet enough
to rhyme; or to angels, or other flying anomaly that shoulders

us above the laterals of the days-in and days-out that numb us
to a ground we have audacity to name and call ours. Shoulders

we have held, elegant boat of bones, that triumvir of ligament,
bone and tendon we teach to lift us into dance. And, shoulders

of children still intact when you saw them last, their baring
holding in their stories and their stories' battered shoulders.

WHAT DO YOU WANT TO BE TRUE, acrylic and graphite on canvas, 32" x 24" MMXX

THE COMPANY OF HORSES

>   —   Why did you leave the horse alone?
>   —   To keep the house company, my son.
>   ~MAHMOUD DARWISH

Left alone they will follow tree lines or fence lines, or any courses
keeping them from whatever's on the other side. I live by horses

in the nearby fields. I run past them every day on my morning run.
My wife takes pictures of her favorite ones and talks to the horses

knowing they know something we're not sure they know. Not
verbs or nouns, or syntax, but something of the timbre horses

know of company, something of the tone of company. I hear them
when other horses pass by in trailers off to some place the horses

in these pastures will not travel to. I do not know the language
of *whinny* but I do not doubt that there is something in horses

pitch being said about need and love and kinship and wanting
company. Cows, goats, crows, geese, lambs living with horses,

and chickens, pigeons and doves and bees know more than
we think they do. Chagall knew lambs. Picasso knew horses.

Look at the village dreams of the one and terror of bombings
in the other. In all the places you live in, look for the horses.

THE DEEP END, acrylic on canvas, 26" x 20" MMXX

THE GUARD

Later Hertzl wrote: *If you divide death by life, you will find a circle*.

My name is Hertzl Shaul, part-time prison guard, on Bassam's side
from early on. I fell in love with numbers as a child. *If you divide*

death by life, you will find a circle is the mathematician inside me,
me thinking of being in the mind of my friend. His smile he'd divide

by something deep within him, then turn it into enigmatic stare.
It made the other guards want to beat the teenager more, divide

him from whatever Arab shit gave him strength, from those mental
patterns he could go to in the perforated ceiling tiles. He'd divide

the tiny holes in the tiles into suits, play endless games of solitaire,
merit extra beating. For him a reckoning of strategies, how to divide

them against themselves. When Abir lay dying I went to see him.
I separated myself from my kippah, went in to witness the *divide*

I had written about earlier not even knowing what I was writing
then. Salwa was with him. Rami, Nurit, Elik, others too. Divide

nothing and you might never get to hold your friend's shoulder
in his grief or enter the mysterious calculus of crossing the divide.

ANGELS PLAYING ON THE GROUND, acrylic on canvas, 26" x 20" MMXXI

AND THEN HE FLEW

> The walker felt a tug and then he was lifted from
> the wire up in the air, arms apart, flying away from
> Mount Zion, out over the hills of Beit Jala.

I was three. I was on my father's shoulders. He remembers the hug
of my tiny hands on his forehead, he says. He says he feels the tug

of that day often, in the office, riding his bike to meet the monks
and others at Beit Jala, when he sees his friend and feels the tug

of friendship that the horrors have brought them to. When death
happens exactly no one knows. We say we see it in that last tug

of breath finally letting go. Some say death's about brain or heart,
their last work inside us and then they're off the job. With a tug

of string or press of buttons the suicide bombers ended all our
lives. The world will never know. How we live on inside the tug

of what was, we have nothing to do with or everything to do with.
Believers know exactly where Muhammad flew to. There's no tug

of this or that in belief. But where Petit flew that day, wired as he
was, the watchers did not know. My father says he feels the tug

of flight sometimes in the turns on those winding roads he takes
to see his friend. It's just him leaning into memory's insistent tug.

SLEEPER'S RIDDLE, acrylic on canvas, 36" x 24" MMXX

FOUND SONG FROM CHECKPOINT 300

Every knot can be untied.

I wanted to tell him that he could turn the lines on himself, a lot
of what they said was double edged. Let's start with *every knot*

can be untied. Untie whatever in your throat reduces us to some-
thing other. Let us start there. Untie the way you see us. Knot

whatever it is in you that sees in me a leopard that *doesn't change
its spots*. Tie that one in a ball. Throw it far away from the knot

in you that makes you call that pregnant woman in the line
a (unintelligible) watermelon. You become angry at the knot

in my keffiyeh I can't unknot, call it *a (unintelligible) dishtowel*.
What *am I, a goat?* Whose voice is in that line? Is it my knot

or yours driving these *looping lyrics?* You say to her *Take off
your veil*, and to me *Lift it. Your undershirt too, asshole.* Knot

that is my heart, the gall under it, whatever knar in the pit
of my stomach, tangle in us untranslatable. I know the knot

in my beads that keeps worry in its place. I know my beads
are in my pocket. I'm asking how to loose our riddled knot.

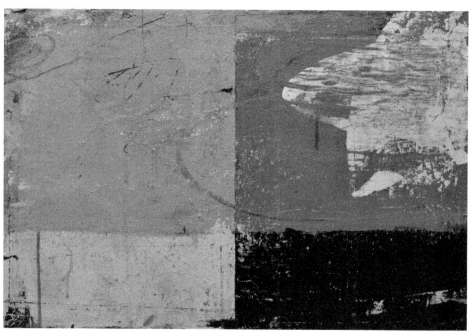

BIRD OF SHADOWS, acrylic on canvas, 16" x 24" MMXIII

SANCTUARY

The hills of Jericho are a bath of dark.

Between the hills and into his garden the spaces fill with lark
song. The Crested Lark and the Desert Lark possess the dark

hours, singing to each other even as he thinks he's pretty sure
birds might sing to us but not for us. Yet tonight in fallen dark

he'll take the notes, the pauses, and play of phrase on phrase.
He'll let them in. Whatever bird intent might be, it's this dark

song calls him out of himself and that's good enough. Inside
the song he's pretty sure now the birds do not sing any dark

thing to anyone. Bird song is a bird thing. The rubber bullets
hit their mark, a Michael falls in Ferguson, a man clad in dark

darker than his outer gear holds a knee in place and breath
ceases. He says he's doing what he was taught, that dark

and evil have to be separated from light and good and that
he was trained to make this call. Geography is often a dark

incidental. Death is death. Murder, murder. What we hear
after is never as it was. Even those birds singing in the dark.

THE VOICE OVER THE FIELD, acrylic on canvas, 36" x 5o" MMIX

WE'LL GATHER AT THE RIVER

Rumi, the poet, the Sufi, said something I will never forget:
Beyond right and wrong there is a field, I'll meet you there.

Travel by wagon, or hack, or caravan or vardo, and wheeled
tracks are part of who you are. You move into woods, a field,

a copse, a meadow. It's yours if you are there. A place is never
really owned in the way you figure things. Greens in the field

next to the stream have negotiated ownership with no one.
Reeds brush unashamedly against women washing or a field

hand coming in from a long day's work or you splashing nearby
with your brothers. Your fathers and uncles in the nearby field

are reciting Rumi. Men and women measure time in *palmas*.
They lose who they are in circling dances. Your voice in a field

with ghazal after ghazal coming through you is your song going
the way wind or rain goes into geographies, one poem as field

guide to another, the next one another guide, and so the next.
It's as though your life depended on you being in the one field

you never knew you could travel to, but there you are, beyond
right and wrong. You're hitching rides from field to field to field.

THE FORTUNE TELLER'S BIRD, acrylic on canvas, 60" x 40" MMXX

NIGHT FLIGHT

Some of the birds migrate at night to avoid predators,
flying in their sidereal patterns, elliptic with speed,
devouring their own muscles and intestines in flight.

Jane Pittman was Ticey before she was Jane. She was some other
name before but she never knew that name. She tried to migrate

to Ohio after the Emancipation. She called it walking. She walked
in circles. Maria Chavez saw her son beheaded. He would migrate

the next day and then he would send for her. The deal went bad.
The deal went bad meant she no longer had a son. Birds migrate

at night, some of them. Maria tied everything she could carry
in an old *jorongo*. After dusk the children who would migrate

were the children who could walk. She would leave the others
with her mother, walk zigzag, forget hunger, sip water, migrate

with others on the path for short periods and then leave them.
From overhead the people in the Darién Gap do not migrate

if you have to see migration to believe it. The trail is winding,
muddy, vine-choked, canopied. They dream of eating, migrate

the way birds do, and butterflies, buffalo, fish, trees, brothers.
You have to know what Harriet knew, bone deep, to migrate.

AUTUMN QUEEN, acrylic on canvas, 24" x 30" MMXIX

EID AL-ADHA

Apeirogon: a shape with a countably infinite number of sides.

She rubs the lamb flanks with spices, with rosemary, sage, tarragon
as she does every *Eid al-Adha*. Belief shapes itself as an apeirogon,

maybe inside her, maybe outside, belief as countable as yesterdays
on days like today. Belief is like the man she married, an apeirogon

who houses love in countless ways. She knows tonight he will cross
the gate to come to sit with her. He will come out of that apeirogon

his study is. He will circle in her circle now. She cuts peppers, grinds
the peppercorns, seeds the pomegranate, another rubied apeirogon

right there before her. Everywhere she's ever lived she's planted
a garden. It was one way to keep going. She knew the apeirogon

grief would bring her daughter to her today. She holds the knife
of sacrifice. She hears her child practicing lessons, this apeirogon

this time as memory with multiplication tables in it and a candy
bracelet. What she hears is round and clear as song, apeirogon

of the geography she lives in telling her to drop the knife. She
scores the lamb, measures her wealth, sings a new apeirogon.

APPENDIX

The following is a guide to the epigraphs used in the poems taken from the hardcover edition of the Colum McCann novel *Apeirogon*: title, canto number, page number; < indicates the canto in the ascending order in the narrative, > indicates the canto in the descending order. Note: the phrases, motives, motifs often appear in variations as phrases, motives, and motifs appear in musical compositions. Notations here are sometimes to one of the appearances of one of the variations of the epigraph.

AFTERWORD
COLUM MCCANN

THAT'S OUR MUSIC

My life was forever changed on a rainy November afternoon in 2015 when I walked up a staircase in the town of Beit Jala in the West Bank. There I met Bassam Aramin and Rami Elhanan, and they told me their stories of the deaths of their daughters in tragic circumstances in Jerusalem, ten years apart.

The two men, one Israeli, one Palestinian, had become friends against all expectations. They explained how they were learning to harness the power of their grief in their lives, and I knew, immediately, that my own life would never be the same. Suddenly all the oxygen was gone from the air.

I had discovered the word apeirogon a few years earlier and I had tucked it into the dark back pocket of my mind. It was an odd and obscure mathematical term representing a shape with a countably infinite number of sides, approaching a circle but never quite reaching its end. It also suggested to me the intricate network of connections that make up the world, and it made me think not only of beauty and community, but also a terrifying sense of complicity.

Every story is an apeirogon. We are all deeply involved with one another whether we know it or not. In that small office in Beit Jala I was moved to tears by the deaths of Abir and Smadar, but I also knew that I was involved in their lives – and their deaths – somehow. My silence. My taxes. My longing. My grief. My belief in the power of storytelling.

When I began writing *Apeirogon*, I had a feeling that it would extend itself into the world. Like Rami and Bassam, I didn't want the story to end. I wanted it to become a sort of Scheherazade tale, a ruse in the face of death, an ongoing celebration of life, a song. I wanted a musician to create his or her own apeirogon. I wanted a poet to create his or her own shape.

I wanted a reader to do it too. In other words, I wanted Abir and Smadar to be entirely alive in the vast expanse of us all.

Darrell Bourque's poems have extended the apeirogon and given even further life to Abir and Smadar. I am stunned and humbled that a poet of such stature would take my words and shape them into something so new and beautiful – something, in fact, profoundly more beautiful. I read these poems, one a day, over the course of weeks – and they gave great grace to my days.

Now another poet, or another musician, or another artist will come to Darrell's poems, paired with the brilliant paintings by Bill Gingles, and they too will extend the apeirogon forever, inwards and outwards, inwards and outwards, inwards and outwards. I can hear two very young girls take a sharp breath.

Words beat death. That's their music.

ACKNOWLEDGEMENTS

First to Bill Gingles. After having completed three collaborations with him (*Where I Waited, From the Other Side-Henriette Delille,* and *migraré*), he invited, no, urged, a fourth collaboration. I had no idea where such a collaboration might take me, us. I thank Bill whose only credit ever in these collaborations, and only royalty, is in the fact that the pairing of his remarkable paintings exist next to a set of poems telling a story of human resilience, human strength, a story that asks that we care and that we take responsibility for what we do in the world.

Then came Colum McCann's *Apeirogon*, with the disarming narratives of Rami Elhanan and Bassam Aramin: their lives and terrible beauty of their marriages, loss, grief, grit, and dignity. The courage and clarity in the lives of Nurit and Salwa is the feminine agency I witness daily in my wife's negotiation with being. The fragile and precious tenderness in Smadar and Abir and their sisters and brothers criss-cross geopolitical boundaries and reside now in my daughters Nicole and Rachel as their stories become our stories. *Apeirogon* gave me a way to respond to Bill.

I thank Colum for his generosity in giving me his story to create another story. In his offering there were no guidelines, restrictions, impediments, or qualifications, only the opening of a new path to the stories that must be told wherever human life and human dignity hang in the balance. *Apeirogon* is his ruse against death with echoes of the ancient tales we recognize in the great epics, the great tales of terror and the struggle for fair play wherever they happen: in India, in Persia, in Greece, in Myanmar, in Charleston South Carolina, in Monroe Louisiana, in Jerusalem, in Jericho, in Minneapolis, in Paris ... wherever.

I want to thank my fellow poets and storytellers who are my teachers and guides. I am always writing alongside them: my fellow Louisiana laureates Brenda Marie Osbey, Ava Haymon, Julie Kane, Jack Bedell, Peter Cooley, John Warner Smith, and Mona Lisa Saloy. My Louisiana French laureates Barry Ancelet, Zachary Richard, and Kirby Jambon. And Jean

Arceneaux, Alison Pelegrin, Martha Serpas, Ashley Mace Havrid and David Havrid, Melissa Bonin, Brad Richard, Sheryl St. Germain, Luis Urrea, Frank Walker, Naomi Shihab Nye, David Kirby, Faisal Mohyuddin, and Yusef Komunyakaa. And the beloveds, Van K. Brock, Randall Kenan and Ernest J. Gaines.

Thanks to the great humanists at Louisiana Endowment for the Humanities who have always supported my work. Also to Jim Davis, Rebecca Hamilton, and Robert Wilson at the Louisiana State Library and the Louisiana Center for the Book, to Marcia Gaudet and Cheylon Woods at the Ernest J. Gaines Center at the University of Louisiana at Lafayette., to George and Rita Marks and all the artists, writers, and volunteers at NuNu's Arts and Culture Collective of Arnaudville.

I am immensely grateful for being included in the mission and outreach programs of the international youth story exchange, Narrative 4, especially to Executive Director and co-founder Lisa Consiglio, whose genius and open-heartedness has created an amazing organization that reimagines the roads to understanding, insight, agency, human dignity, and human rights through the telling of stories. I am grateful to her leaders and facilitators: Gregory Khalil, Lee Keylock, Karen Hollins, Heather Mitchell, Gideon Stein, Hillary Wells, Felice Belle, Margaret LaRaia, Elissa Schappell, Ru Freeman, Ishmael Reah, Rob Spillman, Buchi Onyegbule, Colm Mac Con Iomaire, Charles Miles, Assaf Gavron, Marlon James, Terry Tempest Williams, Ruth Gilligan, Lila Azam Zanganeh, to the youth and their teachers, especially Thalia, Lily, Malak, Alex, Genti, Uri, Yamsi, Bobsie, to Mary Slone, Hazel Joseph Roseboro, Lillian de Jesus and their students at University Heights in the Bronx and Floyd County Century High in eastern Kentucky, and to Narrative 4's regional directors and facilitators and storytellers throughout the United States, in Ireland, Africa, Mexico, Israel, Palestine, and other sites where the organization brings the work of radical empathy into schools, communities, families. And, of course, to co-founder of the global non-profit, Colum McCann.

And finally, to my wife Karen. You inform every poem I have ever written. Your patience as I withdraw into a book like this one, your anticipation of the new poems as they are made, your careful and loving reading. Your support throughout my life, your partnership. I cannot begin to tell you how you make me see, how you help me to find my way through the poems, and then how to take these poems into our everyday lives together.

Darrell Bourque
November 2021

Since the paintings preceded the poems, let me first express my deepest gratitude to my wife Diana. She is my joy and my muse. Her love for me is the solid ground I live on. I cannot count the number of days and nights over the years she has spent alone because I was in the studio painting. She has always believed in me. When I have questioned the validity or value of my paintings, she has come to their defense. Without her, these paintings wouldn't exist or, at best, wouldn't look like they do here. That pretty much goes for me, too.

And to Darrell. I am so grateful for our friendship. We're like brothers from different mothers. Working together, poet and painter, on this book has been a real challenge but it's definitely one of the most important things I've done in my life. Seeing my paintings stand next to your luminous poems is inspiring. Thank you for a beautiful experience.

Bill Gingles
November 2021

About The Author

Darrell Bourque is a descendent of the Acadians who migrated to Louisiana in the 18th century, and he holds some hope that the trace of First Nations peoples' blood in his DNA might be a connection to Mi'kmaq ancestry as well. He was born in Church Point, Louisiana in 1942, a son of farmers and laborers.

He attended University of Louisiana-Lafayette and Florida State University. He has taught in both high schools and at university. At UL Lafayette he served as Director of the Deep South Writers Conference, the Director of Freshman English, Director of Creative Writing, and Coordinator of UL's Interdisciplinary Humanities Program. He ended his tenure there as Head of the English Department.

He served as the president of the National Association for Humanities Education (now HERA- Humanities Education Research Association) and was the editor of *Interdisciplinary Humanities*, the journal of the national organization. He is the recipient of the Louisiana Center for the Book's Louisiana Book Festival Writer Award, the William Rivers Prize in Louisiana Studies, and in 2019 was named the Louisiana Endowment for the Humanities Humanist of the Year Award. He served two terms as Louisiana Poet Laureate (2007-2011). He is a founder and advisory board member of the Ernest J. Gaines Center on the campus of UL Lafayette and is one of the founders of Narrative 4, an international youth story exchange. He is also on the advisory board of Festival of Words of Grand Coteau, Louisiana, a poetry program designed to serve rural and underserved students and the communities they live in. Since its inception Festival of Words has brought in at least one national poetry figure, among them Naomi Shihab Nye, Randall Kenan, Cornelius Eady, Sheryl St. Germain, Toi Derricotte, Patricia Smith, and Tim Seibles.

Darrell Bourque's last four books have been collaborations with Shreveport, Louisiana abstract expressionist artist Bill Gingles.

About the Artist

Bill Gingles is an artist and former art educator. His paintings are represented by galleries in the US, British Columbia, and London. His work is in private and corporate collections in the US, Canada, Mexico, and the UK. He works and lives in Louisiana with his wife Diana and their three Jack Russell terriers: Bridget, Farley, and Penny.

Books from Etruscan Press

Voodoo Libretto: New and Selected Poems | Tim Seibles
Rough Ground | Alix Anne Shaw
A Heaven Wrought of Iron: Poems From the Odyssey | D. M. Spitzer
American Fugue | Alexis Stamatis
Variations in the Key of K | Alex Stein
The Casanova Chronicles | Myrna Stone
Luz Bones | Myrna Stone
In the Cemetery of the Orange Trees | Jeff Talarigo
The White Horse: A Colombian Journey | Diane Thiel
The Arsonist's Song Has Nothing to Do With Fire | Allison Titus
Bestiality of the Involved | Spring Ulmer
Silk Road | Daneen Wardrop
The Fugitive Self | John Wheatcroft
YOU. | Joseph P. Wood

Etruscan Press Is Proud of Support Received From

Wilkes University

Youngstown State University

Ohio Arts Council

The Stephen & Jeryl Oristaglio Foundation

Community of Literary Magazines and Presses [clmp]

National Endowment for the Arts

Drs. Barbara Brothers & Gratia Murphy Endowment

The Thendara Foundation

Founded in 2001 with a generous grant from the Oristaglio Foundation, Etruscan Press is a nonprofit cooperative of poets and writers working to produce and promote books that nurture the dialogue among genres, achieve a distinctive voice, and reshape the literary and cultural histories of which we are a part.

etruscan press

www.etruscanpress.org

Etruscan Press books may be ordered from

Consortium Book Sales and Distribution
800.283.3572
www.cbsd.com

Etruscan Press is a 501(c)(3) nonprofit organization.
Contributions to Etruscan Press are tax deductible
as allowed under applicable law.
For more information, a prospectus,
or to order one of our titles,
contact us at books@etruscanpress.org.